JUST AROUND THE CORNER

POEMS BY
JAMES STEVENSON
WITH ILLUSTRATIONS
BY THE AUTHOR

GREENWILLOW BOOKS
An Imprint of HarperCollins*Publishers*

Watercolor paints and a
black pen were used to
prepare the full-color art.
Just Around the Corner: Poems
Copyright © 2001
by James Stevenson
All rights reserved. Printed in
Hong Kong by South China
Printing Co. (1988) Ltd.
www.harperchildrens.com

Library of Congress
Cataloging-in-Publication Data

Stevenson, James, (date)
Just around the corner:
poems / by James Stevenson.
      p.   cm.
"Greenwillow Books."
Summary: A collection of short
poems on a variety of topics,
including "Classroom," "After
the Storm," and "Tow Truck."
ISBN 0-688-17303-9 (trade).
ISBN 0-06-029189-3 (lib. bdg.)
1. Children's poetry, American.
[1. American poetry.] I. Title.
PS3569.T4557 J87 2001
811'.54—dc21   00-022547

First Edition
10 9 8 7 6 5 4 3 2

For Harvey, with love

CONTENTS

Umbrellas   7

After the Storm   8

Machine   11

Classroom   12

Tanker   14

The No-More Diner   16

The Fold-Up Dock   19

Which Is the Best?   20

Two Old Signs, Cape Cod   22

Dead-Low Tide   24

Trees   26

Cookies   27

My Underwood Typewriter   28

Good for Grapes   31

La Fabulosa   33

Old Shoes   34

The Irish Cake   37

Fan   38

The Fairbanks Scale   41

December Sunday   42

Matt on the Subway   45

Plows   47

Why?   48

Tow Truck   50

House   53

Windowsill   54

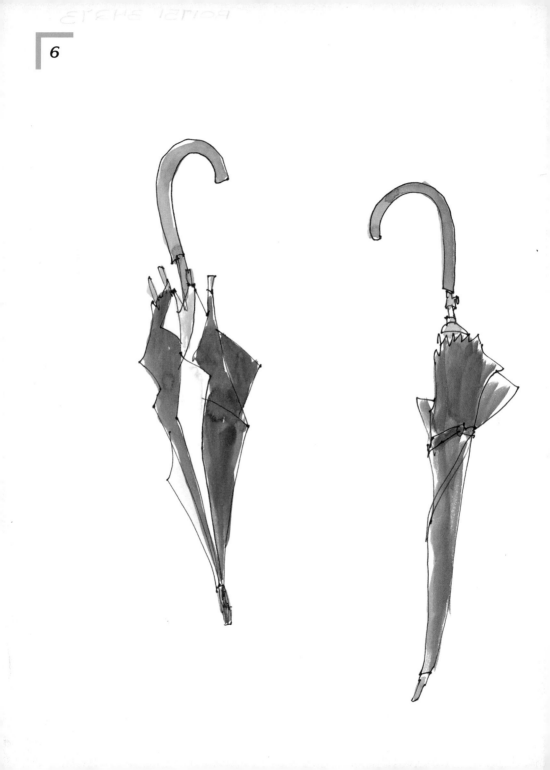

What must umbrellas

think of the world?

Every time they go outside,

it's raining.

After the storm, we'd run down the block

Kicking frozen hunks of slush

From wheels of cars.

If you kicked it right,

And you were lucky,

The hunk would crash to the street

In one huge piece:

KA-CHUNK!

**Before they invented this,
I wonder how many people it took
To do the job?**

WHEN I RAISED MY HAND IN CLASS,

IT DIDN'T MEAN I KNEW THE ANSWER.

FAR FROM IT.

I WAS HOPING THE ANSWER MIGHT FLOAT BY.

AND I COULD CATCH IT LIKE A BUTTERFLY.

Here's the oil tanker coming up the river.

Anybody need a few thousand gallons?

Fill 'er up!

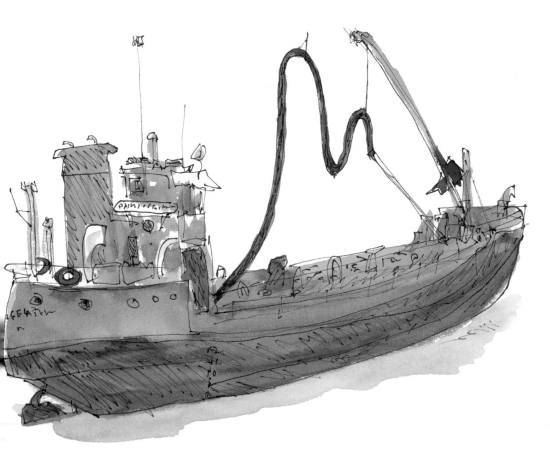

No more **cole slaw**

No more **fries**

No more **coffee**

No more **giant menus**

No more **hot soup**

No more **cold ice cream**

No more **crashing china**

No more **noisy talk**

No more **pink booths of Naugahyde...**

It's the **No-More Diner** *now ...*

Memories to Go.

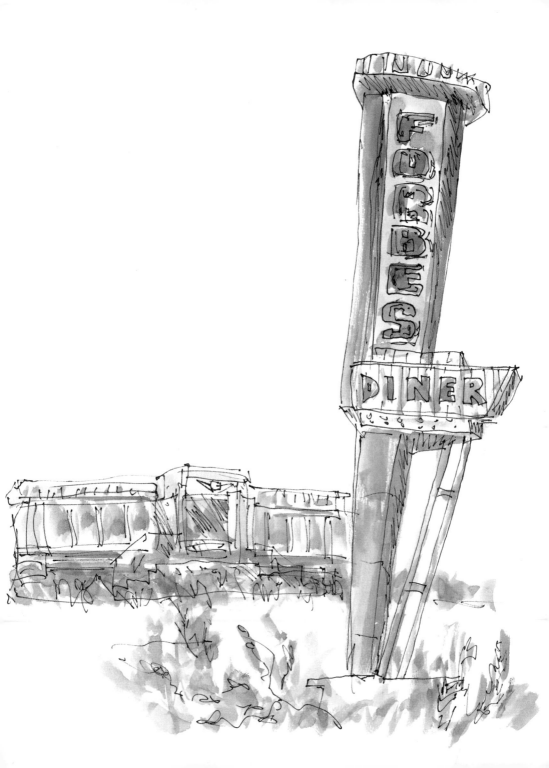

Who lives in this cabin on the side of a cliff?

What does he do with his fold-up dock?

Maybe he's an old pirate, watching the river with his one good eye,

In case of visitors.

If he sees a boat, he darts outside

And cranks the screeching boom, hauling up his dock.

Then he goes inside, slams the door,

And peers through his dusty window,

A gold tooth gleaming in his black beard.

Ice cream on a stick,

Covered with cold, shiny chocolate,

Or ice cream heaped up in a cone,

Dripping fast on a hot day,

Or ice cream in a big blue bowl
And a spoon you can take your time with—

Which is the best?

It is too soon
To give the answer.

I have more testing
To do.

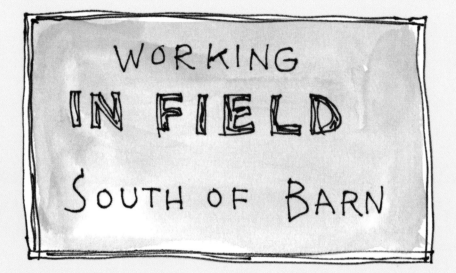

WORKING
IN FIELD
NORTH OF BARN

You'd never see it
Unless you were slopping around
At dead-low tide:
The old tire, sunk in the mud,
Growing its own green seaweed and barnacles,
Trying not to be noticed.

*T*he Christmas captives

Tied with twine

Lean against each other on the city sidewalk,

Whispering of the frozen woods back home.

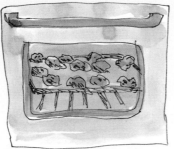

COOKIES
BAKING

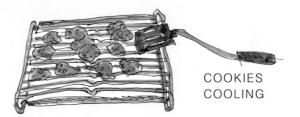

COOKIES
COOLING

COOKIES
READY

COOKIES GONE

```
I lo ve my old underwood typewriter
I ju st wish it worke d a litt le better
```

Children never argue over grapes.

They're all the same size,

There are plenty of them, and

They all taste sweet.

La Fabulosa Grocery . . .

What a splendid name!

It makes you wonder

Why in the world

Anyone would name their grocery

Shop-Rite, or **A&P**.

Tough as nails,

They've been around . . .

Snow, sleet, mud, sand, ice . . .

Scraped, battered, wrinkled, gnarled,

Worn-down, fixed-up, split apart,

Re-soled, re-heeled . . .

Now it's time for them to rest indoors,

Next to the softies:

The bedroom slippers,

The sandals,

The shower-shoes.

The recipe was Irish, and we left it in too long,

And the cake came smoking out of the oven

Like a crusty chunk of bog,

Bristling with burnt-black raisins,

Ready to fight . . .

And when we tried to slice a piece,

The brute erupted, spraying crumbs across the kitchen . . .

But, oh, what a taste it had,

Sweet as names like Killarney, Donegal, Athlone.

Long before air conditioners
Stuck their snouts out city windows,
Groaning over their work,

This plucky, streamlined electric fan

Took the edge off August.

Don't try to fool the Fairbanks.

The Fairbanks knows.

Oh, you can step right up

In your birthday suit,

Saying, "Bet I've lost a couple of pounds,"

But the cranky, clanking Fairbanks only murmurs,

"Guess you forgot that raisin cookie!

How about that cherry pie?"

It's a warm Sunday in December,
And the beach fills up again
As if it were July.

carrying
is back

staring is back

yapping
is back

Grandmas
are back

beach
balls
are
back

strollers
are back

reading
is back

romance
is back

dogs with
sticks are back

exploring is back

beach pails
and shovels
are back

tourists
are back

leashes
are back

waiting for
somebody to
throw the ball
is back

beach chairs, beer bottles,
and cell phones are back

cameras
are
back

digging
is back

newspapers
are back

wading
is back

music is back

Master of the thundering subway train,

Matt stands steady at the helm,

Looking out the front window

At the shiny tracks, the colored lights,

The dark tunnels whirling past,

And if he gives any command at all,

It's probably, *"Faster!"*

The radio said snow all night,

But now it's 6 A.M. and nothing yet.

The snowplows wait outside the diner,

Engines running, ready for takeoff;

The drivers huddle inside,

Warming their hands and feet,

Taking on coffee,

Watching the windows

For the flakes to fall.

Why is it . . .
While other people
Are thinking about all kinds of
Important things . . .
I am thinking about
What it would be like
To jump barefoot
Into an open box
Of jelly doughnuts?

It's got a few more rescues left,

A few more icy Interstates in fog and snow,

But not too many, probably.

Then a newer tow will come

And haul this one

Away.

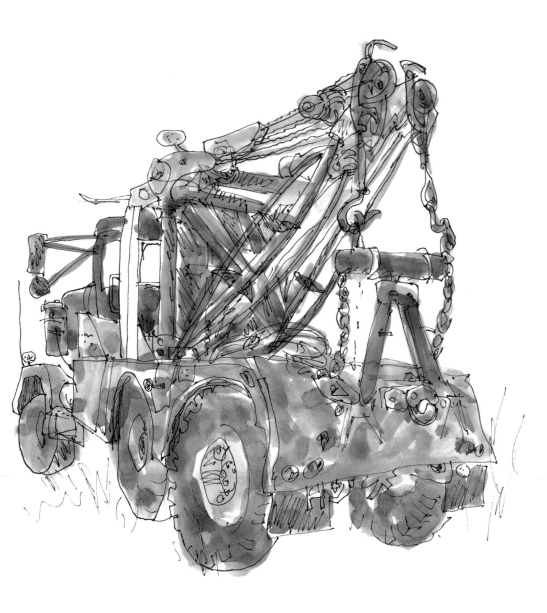

*P*EOPLE BUY OLD HOUSES HERE,

THEN KNOCK THEM DOWN

TO BUILD A BIGGER ONE.

THIS HOUSE WAS NEARLY GONE

WHEN THE HOLIDAYS ARRIVED.

NOW IT HAS TO WAIT,

OPEN TO THE RAIN AND SNOW

IT ONCE KEPT OUT.

On the windowsill in the kitchen
There's a bottle that once held tea,
A pot of chopsticks,
Some cactus,
A feather,
A metal grasshopper,
A wooden cardinal,
A spoon,
A jar of sea lavender,
A stone,
A wishbone,
And a piece of sea glass.

When winter closes in, cold and gray,
You can look no farther
Than this windowsill
And think of
Hot tea,
Spicy food,
Desert places where the sun is pouring down,
Birds soaring,
Creatures jumping in the tall grass come summer,
Dishes of ice cream,
Salt marshes in bloom,
Wishes not yet wished,
And green waves crashing on a white beach.